Franz Josef Goetz

Privatization in Ukraine: Conclusions from TACIS experience

GRIN Verlag

Bibliografische Information der Deutschen Nationalbibliothek:

Die Deutsche Bibliothek verzeichnet diese Publikation in der Deutschen National-
bibliografie; detaillierte bibliografische Daten sind im Internet über http://dnb.d-
nb.de/ abrufbar.

Dieses Werk sowie alle darin enthaltenen einzelnen Beiträge und Abbildungen
sind urheberrechtlich geschützt. Jede Verwertung, die nicht ausdrücklich vom
Urheberrechtsschutz zugelassen ist, bedarf der vorherigen Zustimmung des Verla-
ges. Das gilt insbesondere für Vervielfältigungen, Bearbeitungen, Übersetzungen,
Mikroverfilmungen, Auswertungen durch Datenbanken und für die Einspeicherung
und Verarbeitung in elektronische Systeme. Alle Rechte, auch die des auszugsweisen
Nachdrucks, der fotomechanischen Wiedergabe (einschließlich Mikrokopie) sowie
der Auswertung durch Datenbanken oder ähnliche Einrichtungen, vorbehalten.

Imprint:

Copyright © 2001 GRIN Verlag GmbH
Druck und Bindung: Books on Demand GmbH, Norderstedt Germany
ISBN: 978-3-640-51642-1

This book at GRIN:

http://www.grin.com/en/e-book/141301/privatization-in-ukraine-conclusions-from-
tacis-experience

GRIN - Your knowledge has value

Der GRIN Verlag publiziert seit 1998 wissenschaftliche Arbeiten von Studenten, Hochschullehrern und anderen Akademikern als eBook und gedrucktes Buch. Die Verlagswebsite www.grin.com ist die ideale Plattform zur Veröffentlichung von Hausarbeiten, Abschlussarbeiten, wissenschaftlichen Aufsätzen, Dissertationen und Fachbüchern.

Visit us on the internet:

http://www.grin.com/

http://www.facebook.com/grincom

http://www.twitter.com/grin_com

Privatization in Ukraine: Conclusions from TACIS Experience

Dr. Franz J. Goetz[1]

Privatization: A Tool

The European Commission's TACIS program[2] in the country is based on the Partnership and Cooperation Agreement finalized between Ukraine and the European Union on 16th of June 1994. One prime objective of this Agreement – for which privatization plays a fundamental role -- is to develop a sustainable market economy, with the state in its proper role, namely as supporter rather than performer of "commercially viable economic activity".

I personally have learnt to believe in market forces and private sector involvement during 20 years of work on transport projects. A good example are past developments in the OECD world, where transport liberalization and privatization, implemented within a competitive environment and in a regulated technical framework, have enhanced the rational use of resources, stimulated technology change and driven transport internationalization. The result was a visible reduction of national distribution costs as percentage of GDP.

> In summary, privatization in transport is not an end in itself, but rather a means to achieve *efficiency gains* for the national economy and *cost savings for* the final consumer.

Certainly, privatization also results in heavily needed "extraordinary" revenue for the State. However, it would be wrong to consider privatization merely a means of budgetary policy, as this would inevitably lead to an exchange of long-term core assets for a one-time state balance sheet cosmetics.

Privatization: The Progress

Confronting facts and theory, one cannot help to conclude that the privatization process in Ukraine with regard to large enterprise has fallen short of target, from a national as well as from a TACIS program perspective.

I can be very short with the description of the national situation, which is widely known: From 1991 until now, foreign direct investment (FDI) and – as part of it – foreign participation in privatization, has been rather modest. As of end of 2000, only some USD 4 billion of FDI have flown into the country, which compares to several times the amount (some 30 billion) – for example- in neighboring Poland.

Looking even at the larger picture of foreign direct investments carried out worldwide, Ukraine has been able to attract only a marginal annual quota of roughly 0.1% on average. One reason is that strategic, long-termed private investment on concession basis (BOT: build, operate, transfer) in the public utilities and infrastructure sector of Ukraine has not yet reached beyond law making level, or not even.

In short :

- Privatization in Ukraine so far has left a high degree of state ownership. 5 200 medium and large enterprises are still fully or partly state owned. Of course, this figure is no reliable yardstick for discussion, as it does not answer the key question of "how many of these enterprises were representing feasible offers for sale?"
- Where privatization has succeeded, it shows - referring to a most recent enterprise survey conducted by the London Business School and covering 250 Ukrainian medium to large enterprises - that it was predominantly done through sales to local entrepreneurs or companies.

This brings me directly to the EC's TACIS projects on "case by case privatization" launched in 1998 which show similar symptoms.

Privatization: The TACIS Approach

An amount of 3.2 million Euro has been allocated over the past four years for technical assistance within the TACIS program in support of privatization in Ukraine. The projects on "case by case privatization" were expected to deliver policy advice on privatization issues and promote large enterprise privatization through methodological sales support.

Having understood from the past, that highly fragmented mass privatization did not sell control, the major idea behind the "case by case privatization" was to sell – in a most transparent way - majority share packages (controlling stakes!) to strategic investors. Advisors from renowned European banking institutions (contractors) were appointed to provide the following services:

- First of all, to facilitate the privatisation of medium/large enterprises through the *sale of block of shares* to industrial and financial investors. The advisor teams of the various contractors would assist in this context the Ukrainian State Property Fund (SPFU) on
  - o regulatory issues for tender sales, as well as in
  - o the final selection of the enterprise to be put up for auction,
  - o the identification of possible investors,
  - o the tender preparation, announcement & conduct;
- At the same time, they were to provide "on the job training" to Ukrainian professionals from the SPFU as the projects' beneficiary.

In line with the Service Contracts, the contractors received from TACIS a retainer fee for their assistance to the sales process, while a one-time success fee had to be paid in case of successful transaction by the SPFU. The success fee corresponds to usual international practice and should guarantee the involvement of well-recognized international investment banks.

Drawing the balance after over 3 years of project implementation, one might conclude that the TACIS "case by case"" privatization program has been humble in outcome, not only with regard to privatization in general, but also concerning all-European partnership development and integration in particular. Major stumbling blocks to successful privatization have been the problematic investment climate and privatization mechanism.

Privatization: The Mechanism

To talk about the better things first: The TACIS program succeeded in policy advice and methodological support to the SPFU. As major single result, a manual on competitive sales was prepared and implemented, which since then guides the privatization process in the Ukraine.

Unfortunately, there is no rose without a thorn: A series of problems have been encountered during the actual sales process, as can be seen from the following:

- altogether 9 initial candidate projects (enterprises) were selected under the TACIS program for privatization; thereof, only one company – the Lutsk Cardboard Plant was sold to a *domestic* majority investor;
- two other sales, initially started with great expectation, namely Crimean Soda Plant and Khartsysk Pipe Rolling Plant, did not succeed in the first round, though for different reasons. Both tenders were voided in July 2000. Still, however, the efforts of the contractors to privatize them continue and might lead to another round of tenders, although the situation remains rather opaque;
- in the case of Stekloplastic factory, again, the tender was not conducted to the end due to lack of bids;
- regarding Chaerkassy Biscuit factory, it was removed by the Government from the SPFU's list of candidate projects for privatization during the tender process;
- Vinnitsa Oil and Fat Plant again, after the entire tender documentation had been prepared and submitted to SPFU, went into bankruptcy during the process and privatization was stopped;
- in the further case under consideration, Rivneazot Chemicals Plant, which evoked great interest also amongst large international companies, the sales process is running in a circle since the beginning.
- Last but not least, one of the three European Banks contracted by the Commission could not even accomplish a definite selection of enterprises, and the Service Contract was terminated before due after one year.

Altogether, the effectiveness of the TACIS privatization support activities so far seems to be rather modest. Giving an answer for the reasons is difficult, as the problems varied from case to case. The major stumbling blocks were either of economic, technical or political nature, the most salient features being the following:

1. Over-estimation of local preparedness for open sales under tender procedure;
2. Lengthy approval process and lack of attractiveness of listed enterprises: The approval process of final enterprise selection was

4

very time consuming. Few of the companies listed were attractive to strategic investors "at first sight". This was partly due to lack of pre-privatization work done in terms of company audit. Moreover, many companies listed were supposed to sell only minority stakes.

3. Problematic strategic choice of company: In other cases not enough attention had been given to the question of "how the enterprise would fit into the global market". In retrospect, a good example for this might be Kharsysk Pipe Rolling Plant: As former supplier of Gazprom and integral part of the Central-Eastern oil and gas industry, the company is by nature of greater strategic interest for investors from the Russian than from the Western market.

4. Absence of bids: The limited interest shown with regard to most enterprises put on auction certainly is a reflection of the difficult investment climate as well as of what has been mentioned under 2. However, sometimes interest from the side of potential investors was compromised by simply wrong perceptions about the political and security situation in Ukraine.

5. Resistance of company management: Negative attitudes towards privatization were experienced in particular amongst the "blue chips" such as Crimean Soda and Khartsysk Pipe Rolling Plant. Resistance, although of lesser political leverage, was also felt in the case of the successfully privatized Lutsk Cardboard Plant.

> **In short: The more attractive the project, the stronger the resistance towards a majority sale.**

6. Unforeseen political events: The privatization process was halted during the last presidential election campaign from more or less July to November 1999. As a result, several tenders could not be published before February 2000, although documentation was ready in August 1999.

7. Controversial decision making by institutions concerned: The policy decision about which enterprises were to be privatized were frequently modified without little warning and debate, before and during the sales process. This phenomena rendered the tender process in certain major cases particularly unstable and complicated.

8. Negative publicity of local mass media, which affected the general privatization climate.

Ukraine will strongly depend on outside finance for future growth. (Note: Private and corporate bank savings amount to no more than 3% of GDP). In order to streamline the privatization process and accelerate foreign strategic involvement in industrial restructuring and modernization in Ukraine, both
- transparent privatization procedures and
- a clear separation of politics from an agreed technical mechanism of privatization
are required.

Post-Privatisation Performance

In economic terms one may say that privatization has not been achieved until the post-privatization performance of enterprises has been improved in a sustainable way. In other words: Change in ownership (from public to private) is a necessary but not sufficient reform step. Although it is possibly true that the profit motive makes work harder, "it does not make the management necessarily smarter " [3]

In fact, recalling again the earlier mentioned enterprise survey carried out by the London School of Economics, it appears that only minor changes were implemented since 1991 in the privatized companies of Ukraine dominated by local entrepreneurs, in particular regarding issues such as the change of production technology, change of management or disposal/renewal of assets.

More often than not the new ownership did not have or did not apply significant new technology and know-how, falling short of the very objective of privatization, namely to bring about modernization of production and access to new markets. Although useful or even necessary, it is generally not sufficient to only "patch up former production cycles" [4]

This brings me back to what was and is still one of the major tasks of the TACIS initiative: to help identify "global players" as majority stake holders with strategic development interest in the companies to be privatized.

Privatization of large Enterprise: The Way forward?

Asking the question "what should be the right way forward", I find it appropriate to make use of a general policy statement once produced by

UEPLAC, the TACIS funded Ukrainian-European Policy and Legal Advice Centre, which – applied to privatization - could read as follows:

> **Privatization policy should be innovative in its analysis and means, instead of being made of Dogma, since there are no blanket rules for the right way forward.**

Regarding the strategic approach to privatization, there are many arguments in favor of a flexible, "case by case" approach also in future, for the several important reasons:

First of all, the question of *"what to privatize"* -- although largely dictated by economic (feasibility) considerations -- will always require a decision at political level, which in fact can take different shape on the same field from case to case, country to country and from Government to Government, depending on political conviction. For example, until fairly recently the operation of public utility networks was in Europe considered a natural state monopoly.

Secondly, the further question of *"when to privatize"* also can lead to different answers from case to case, depending on the country-specific situation of state finance on the one hand, and possible social implications of change of ownership on the other. There can be however no doubt, that social policy objectives need to be integral part of privatization policies, in order to guarantee sustainability in the longer run.

Remains the final question of *"how to privatize"*. Also here I could imagine, that different organizational strategies might apply to different cases. While it might be the right approach to propose the entire transfer of a viable government enterprise to the private sector in the one case, the breaking-up in separate business units might be the more appropriate approach in others. (For example: In 1984, the telecommunications branch of the former British General Post Office was separately sold as British Telecom).

Reconsidering the slowness of the privatization process in Ukraine, which is partly due weaknesses of the institutional environment or the unattractiveness of listed state enterprises, renewed focus should be possibly on:

- strengthening and improving the institutional framework;

- pre-privatization activities (first fix and then sell!) to clearly articulate the business purpose. Often, the conflicting mix of social, political and business objectives inherited from the past disguises the companies' core business identity.

As finally concerns the technical conduct of open tenders, only one approach can be accepted once the state enterprise is selected and officially put on auction: A guaranteed mechanism of tender process in accordance with the established rules, for not undermining the confidence of the international investors' community in Ukraine's business scene and conduct.

---

[1] Dr. Franz J. Goetz, Economist and Independent Consultant on international technical assistance projects, presented this paper on the occasion of the "XVI Round Table of the Advisory Project of the German Government on Privatization in Ukraine", March 23rd, 2001 – Kiev. The author was at that time Chief Economist at the Delegation of the European Commission in Kiev, Ukraine.

[2] **TACIS** is an abbreviation of "Technical Aid to the Commonwealth of Independent States" program, a foreign and technical assistance program implemented by the European Commission to help members of the Commonwealth of Independent States, in their transition to democratic market-oriented economies.

[3] "W.Pfaff, "The Privatisation of Public Utilities can be a Disaster". In: International Herald Tribune, 22.02.2001

[4] W. Pfaff